Multiplication
at the Market

by Brett Kelly

Table of Contents

Introduction

Many families use **multiplication** at the market. Multiplication is a fast way to add **equal groups**.

I need to know these math words.

equal groups

Multiplication helps people know how much to buy. The families in this book use multiplication. Each family buys food for a special meal.

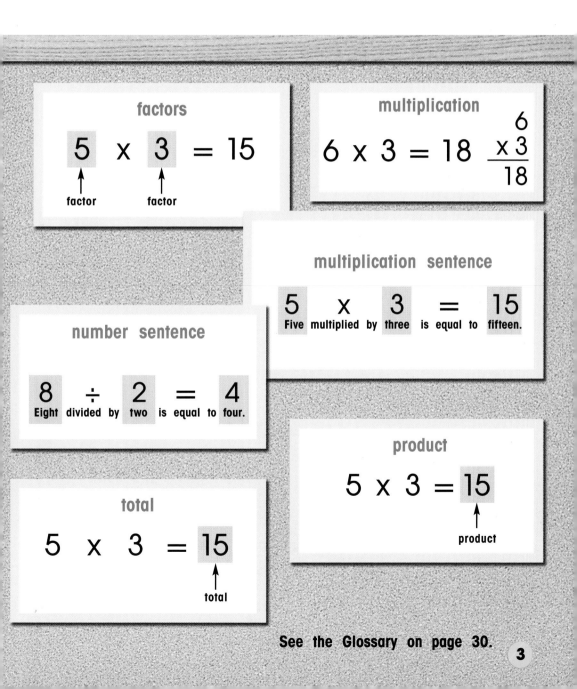

factors

$$5 \times 3 = 15$$

factor   factor

multiplication

$$6 \times 3 = 18 \quad \begin{array}{r} 6 \\ \times\, 3 \\ \hline 18 \end{array}$$

multiplication sentence

$$5 \quad \times \quad 3 \quad = \quad 15$$

Five multiplied by three is equal to fifteen.

number sentence

$$8 \quad \div \quad 2 \quad = \quad 4$$

Eight divided by two is equal to four.

product

$$5 \times 3 = 15$$

product

total

$$5 \quad \times \quad 3 \quad = \quad 15$$

total

See the Glossary on page 30.

How Many for Breakfast?

This family is making French toast for breakfast. The family needs to buy eggs. The family buys two cartons of eggs. Each carton has twelve eggs.

▲ This family needs eggs to make French toast.

The family buys two equal groups of eggs. Each group has twelve eggs. The family buys twenty-four eggs.

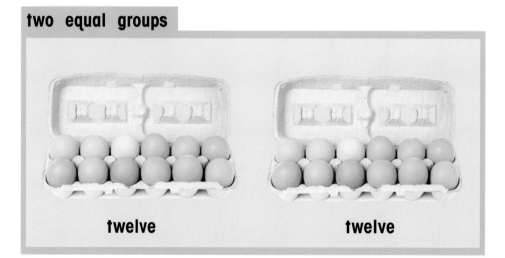

two equal groups

twelve   twelve

▲ The family buys two equal groups. There are twelve eggs in each group. There are twenty-four eggs in all.

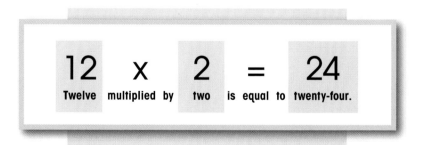

12   x   2   =   24

Twelve   multiplied by   two   is equal to   twenty-four.

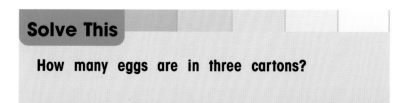

Solve This

How many eggs are in three cartons?

The family also needs to buy bread. The family buys two loaves of bread. Each loaf of bread has ten slices. There are two equal groups. There are ten slices in each group.

two equal groups

ten

ten

What is the **total** number of slices? The family buys twenty slices of bread. The total is twenty slices of bread.

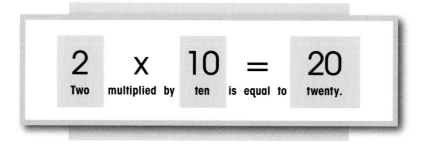

2   x   10   =   20

Two   multiplied by   ten   is equal to   twenty.

Math Talk

Each person wants three slices of French toast. Tell how many slices in all. Will the family have enough bread?

The family likes berries on French toast. The family buys three containers of berries. Each container has seven berries. There are seven berries in each group.

three equal groups

seven

seven

seven

▲ **The family buys berries for the French toast.**

This **number sentence** shows the total.
The total number of berries is twenty-one.
There are twenty-one berries in all.

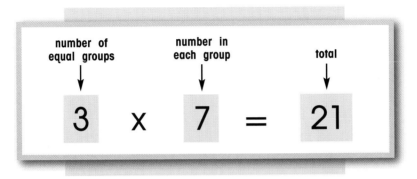

number of equal groups		number in each group		total	
↓		↓		↓	
3	X	7	=	21	

▲ **This number sentence shows how many in all.**

Math Talk

Tell a partner about the number sentence.
Tell how many equal groups you see. Tell
how many are in each group.

How Many for Lunch?

This family is buying food for lunch. The family will make pizzas for lunch. The family will make six pizzas.

▲ This family will make pizzas.

Each pizza has four slices. There are four in each group. How many slices will the family have? The family writes a **multiplication sentence** to find the total.

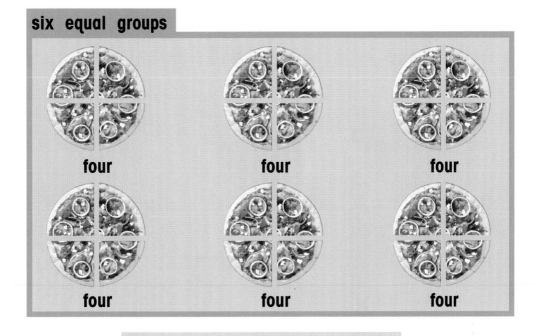

six equal groups

four   four   four

four   four   four

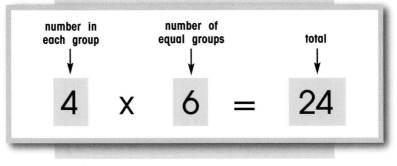

number in each group		number of equal groups		total
↓		↓		↓
4	x	6	=	24

▲ This number sentence shows how many slices.

Math Talk

Talk about the total. Tell how many pizzas you see. Tell how many slices in each pizza. Tell how many slices in all.

The family will make six pizzas. Each pizza will need two cups of sauce. The family will put two cups on each pizza.

six equal groups

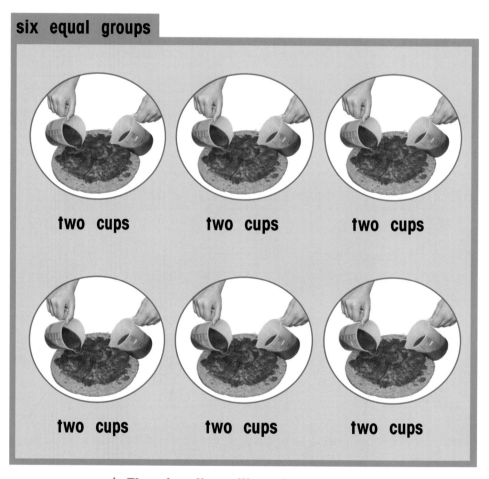

| two cups | two cups | two cups |
| two cups | two cups | two cups |

▲ The family will put sauce on six pizzas.

Solve This

How many cups will the family need in all? Write a multiplication sentence to show how many cups.

The pizzas also need cheese. Each pizza will have five ounces of cheese. How many ounces of cheese will the family need?

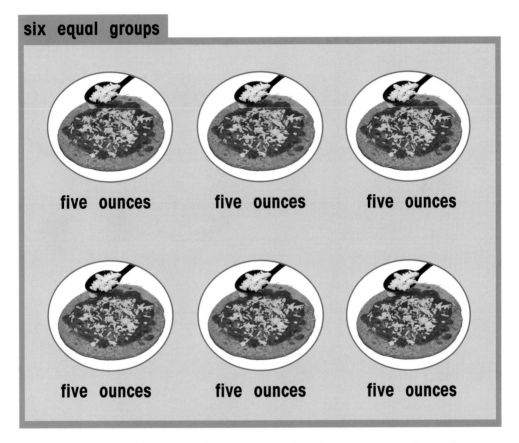

six equal groups

five ounces   five ounces   five ounces

five ounces   five ounces   five ounces

▲ The family will put cheese on six pizzas.

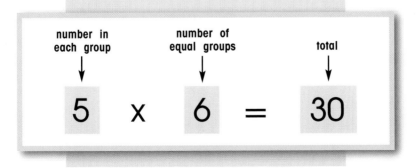

number in each group	number of equal groups	total
↓	↓	↓
5	x 6	= 30

▲ The total is thirty. The family will need thirty ounces of cheese.

Four pizzas will have mushrooms. There are four equal groups. Four is a **factor**. Each pizza will have eight pieces of mushroom. There are eight in each group. Eight is a factor.

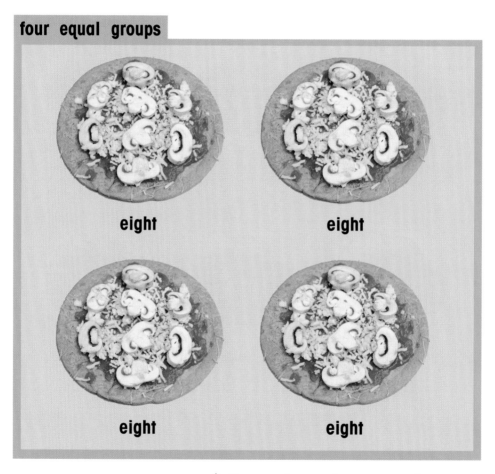

four equal groups

eight   eight

eight   eight

▲ **Four pizzas have mushrooms.**

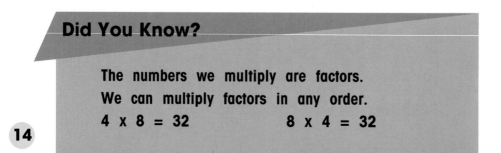

Did You Know?

The numbers we multiply are factors.
We can multiply factors in any order.
4 x 8 = 32   8 x 4 = 32

How many pieces of mushroom will the family need? The family will need thirty-two pieces of mushroom. Thirty-two is the total. Thirty-two is the **product**.

factor   factor   product

4   X   8   =   32

How Many for Dinner?

This family is buying food for dinner. Some friends will eat with the family. The family needs to cook enough food for nine people. The family is cooking chicken, fish, and vegetables.

First, the family needs to buy chicken.
Each pound of chicken makes three pieces.
The family buys four pounds of chicken.
How many pieces can the family make?

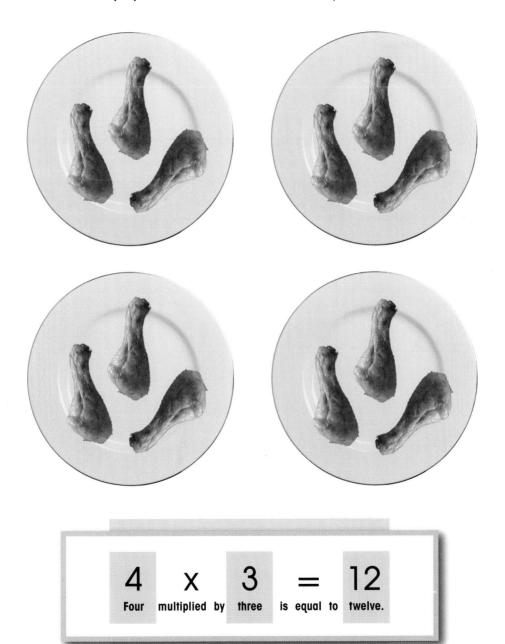

4 x 3 = 12

Four **multiplied by** **three** **is equal to** **twelve.**

Now the family needs to buy some fish. The family buys three pounds of fish. The fish is four dollars per pound. How much does the family pay for fish?

three pounds

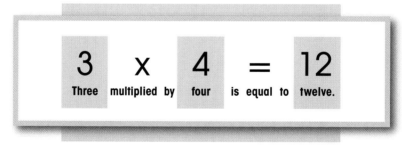

3 x 4 = 12

Three multiplied by four is equal to twelve.

▲ **The family pays twelve dollars for fish.**

Math Talk

Talk about this number sentence. Tell which numbers are factors. Tell what number is the product.

The family will also make shrimp. Each person will have eight shrimp. How many shrimp will the family need in all? Use a multiplication sentence to find out.

9	x	8	=	72
Nine	multiplied by	eight	is equal to	seventy-two.

Math Talk

How many shrimp will the family buy? Tell which numbers are factors. Tell what number is the product.

FRESH ALASKAN SPOT SHRIMP $14.99 POUND

JUMBO GRILLING (U-6) SCAMPI

FRESH LOCAL MUSSELS $2.89 POUND

FRESH MANILA CLAMS GREAT FOR STEAMING $3.99 POUND

The family will make grilled tomatoes. Each person wants three tomatoes. How many tomatoes will the family need? The family writes a number sentence to find out.

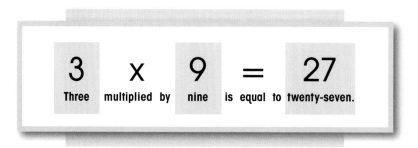

$$3 \times 9 = 27$$

Three multiplied by nine is equal to twenty-seven.

▲ The total is twenty-seven tomatoes. The family will need twenty-seven tomatoes in all.

Some people eat rice. The family buys three bags of rice. Each bag has eight cups of rice. The mother uses multiplication to find the total.

three equal groups

eight cups   eight cups   eight cups

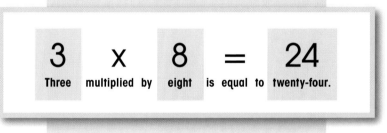

3 x 8 = 24

Three   multiplied by   eight   is equal to   twenty-four.

▲ The product is twenty-four. The total is twenty-four.

Solve This

Each cup of rice is equal to three servings. The family will make six cups for dinner. How many servings will the family make? Which number sentence shows how many servings?

a) 3 x 3 = 9

b) 6 + 6 = 12

c) 3 x 2 = 6

d) 6 + 6 + 6 = 18

How Many for Dessert?

This family will have ice cream for dessert.
Some people like bananas with ice cream.
The family buys three bunches of bananas.
There are three equal groups of bananas.
Three is a factor.

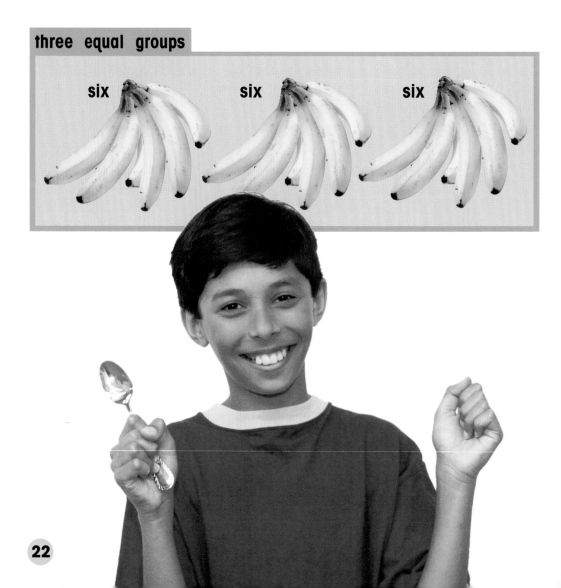

three equal groups

six   six   six

The family has three bunches of bananas. Each bunch has six bananas. There are six bananas in each bunch. Six is a factor. How many bananas does the family buy in all?

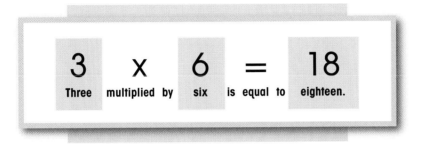

3	x	6	=	18
Three	multiplied by	six	is equal to	eighteen.

▲ The family buys eighteen bananas in all. Eighteen is the product.

Solve This

Each bowl has one banana. How many bowls of ice cream can the family make? Write a number sentence to show how many in all.

Seven people will have ice cream. Each person will have three scoops of ice cream. How many scoops will the people need in all?

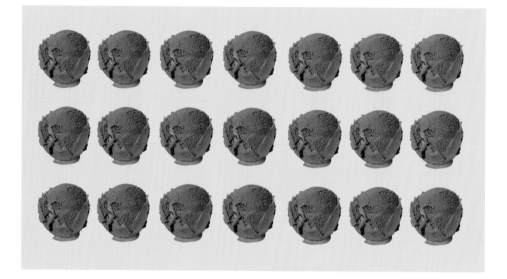

$$7 \quad \times \quad 3 \quad = \quad 21$$

Seven   multiplied by   three   is equal to   twenty-one.

▲ Seven people will have ice cream. Each person will have three scoops.

Solve This

Each container has eight scoops of ice cream. The family buys four containers of ice cream. How many scoops will the family buy in all?

The family buys chocolate sauce for the ice cream. Only six people like chocolate sauce. Each person will get two spoons of chocolate sauce. How many spoons of chocolate sauce will the family need?

▲ Six people want chocolate sauce. The family needs twelve spoons of chocolate sauce.

Math Talk

Work with a partner. Tell how many spoons of chocolate sauce the family will need. Write a multiplication sentence. Tell which numbers are the factors. Tell what number is the product.

Some people like nuts on ice cream. Six people will have nuts. Each person will have nine nuts. How many nuts in all? The son writes a number sentence to find out.

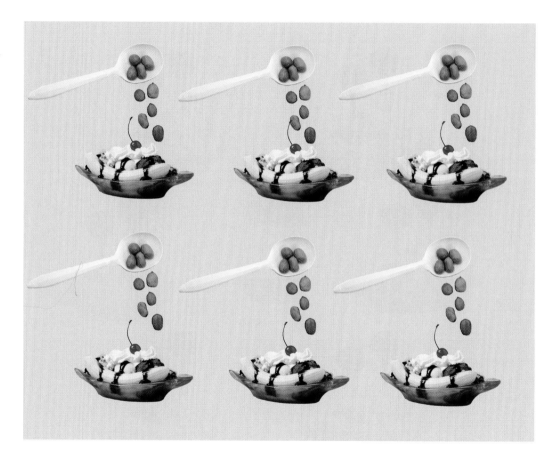

6	x	9	=	54
Six	multiplied by	nine	is equal to	fifty-four.

▲ Six bowls of ice cream have nuts. Each bowl has nine nuts. There are fifty-four nuts in all.

Multiplication Table

X	1	2	3	4	5	6	7	8	9	10	11	12
1	1	2	3	4	5	6	7	8	9	10	11	12
2	2	4	6	8	10	12	14	16	18	20	22	24
3	3	6	9	12	15	18	21	24	27	30	33	36
4	4	8	12	16	20	24	28	32	36	40	44	48
5	5	10	15	20	25	30	35	40	45	50	55	60
6	6	12	18	24	30	36	42	48	54	60	66	72
7	7	14	21	28	35	42	49	56	63	70	77	84
8	8	16	24	32	40	48	56	64	72	80	88	96
9	9	18	27	36	45	54	63	72	81	90	99	108
10	10	20	30	40	50	60	70	80	90	100	110	120
11	11	22	33	44	55	66	77	88	99	110	121	132
12	12	24	36	48	60	72	84	96	108	120	132	144

Page 5:

Three cartons have thirty-six (36) eggs.
12 x 3 = 36 or 3 x 12 = 36

Page 12:

The family will need twelve (12) cups in all.
6 x 2 = 12 or 2 x 6 = 12

Page 21:

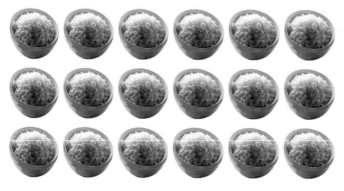

d. 6 + 6 + 6 = 18

Page 23:

The family can make eighteen (18) bowls in all.
18 x 1 = 18 or 1 x 18 = 18

Page 24:

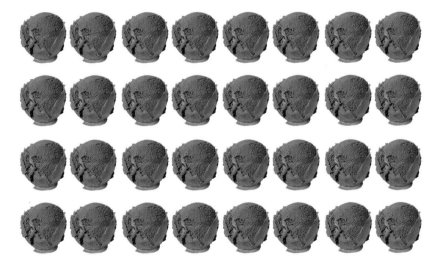

The family buys thirty-two (32) scoops in all.
8 x 4 = 32 or 4 x 8 = 32

Glossary

equal groups groups that have the same number of items

Multiplication is a fast way to add equal groups.

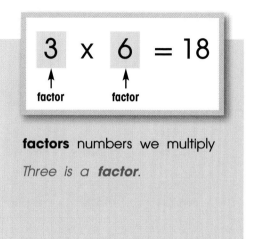

factors numbers we multiply

Three is a factor.

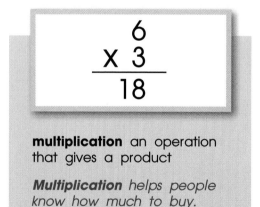

multiplication an operation that gives a product

Multiplication helps people know how much to buy.

$$3 \times 6 = 18$$

multiplication sentence a sentence that includes numbers, x, and =

Use a multiplication sentence to find out.

$$12 + 12 = 24$$

number sentence a sentence that includes numbers and symbols

*This **number sentence** shows the total.*

$$4 \times 8 = \boxed{32}$$
↑
product

product the answer in a multiplication problem

*Thirty-two is the **product**.*

$$10 + 10 = \boxed{20}$$
$$2 \times 10 = \boxed{20}$$
↑
total

total the sum or whole amount

*The **total** is twenty slices of bread.*

Index

After You Read . . .

Multiplication at the Market

Materials:
- price tags in whole dollar amounts, $1–$12, for classroom items

Instructions:

1. Work with a partner.

2. Tell what you want to buy.

3. Tell how many you want to buy.

4. Ask: How much does this item cost?

5. Write a number sentence about the cost.

6. Talk about the cost.